WHY DO BAD
THINGS HAPPEN
TO GOOD
PEOPLE?

Hope, Healing and the
Hidden Purpose Behind Our Pain

JOE T. A. NWOKOYE

ISBN: 979-8-9922738-1-6 (paperback)

Because of the dynamic nature of the Internet, any web addresses or
links contained in this book may have changed since publication and
may no longer be valid. The views expressed in this work are solely those
of the author and do not necessarily reflect the views of the publisher,
and the publisher hereby disclaims any responsibility for them.

INKTRAIL PRESS
CRAFTING STORIES, INSPIRING READERS

CONTENTS

DEDICATION

This small book is dedicated to everyone on this planet who loves Jesus Christ, who died for all our sins. He came to seek and save all who were lost, for all have sinned and come short of the glory of God.

ACKNOWLEDGEMENT

All the glory goes to the Almighty God in whose mighty hands, all lives dwells. Special thanks to my wife Sarah and my children for their great sacrifice and support. To all my partners and friends for their encouragement and support in the call of my life, may the God of Zion bless you and your families.

Finally, to all the Pastors, Deacons, Lecturers, and members of Zion for your prayers and hard work to see the vision fulfilled – Be blessed as you enjoy the covenant we have with Christ Jesus.

FORWARD

Many of us have been experiencing some tough trials and the temptation is to ask the Lord "Why? Why me? Why them?" It's the human nature to ask those questions. But isn't that a victim – oriented question. Are we victims or are we children of God – adopted into His family, protected by his love and race?

My brother Joe Nwokoye has a testimony because he has been tested. Pastor Joe doesn't have the "why" question. Instead Joe have learned that when a trail comes, through the Lord's hands lean into it and ask "father, what does it mean? (Acts 2:12 and what must I do? (Acts 2:37). Those question the Lord always answers – perhaps not initially, but always eventually.

James wrote, "Dear brothers and sisters, when trouble of any kind come your way, consider it an opportunity for great joy. For you know that when your faith is tested, your endurance has a chance to grow. So let it grow, for when your endurance is fully developed, you will be perfect and complete needing nothing" (James1:2-4 NTL)

Maybe you're facing a time of hardship right now. Maybe you've had the bottom drop out in life, and in the midst of your suffering, you're asking, "What is going on? I am a Christian. I am walking with Jesus, yet this difficulty has befallen me. What have I done to deserve this?

If you are going through a time of suffering and difficulty, then this book is for you.

Every Christian will face trials in life – for their own good. Jesus said, "Here on earth you will have many trails and sorrows. But take heart, because I have overcome the world' (john 16:33 NTL). He didn't say you might have trials and sorrows; He said you will have them.

We want to have an emotional mountaintop, but the reality is that spiritual fruit typically does not grow on mountaintops; it grows in the valleys. It grows in the time of suffering and difficulty. In Isaiah 43, God said, "For I am about to do something new. See, I have already begun! Do you see it? I will make a pathway through the wilderness. I will create rivers in the dry wasteland" (verse 19 NTL)

It's in the wasteland, in the hardships, in the difficulties that I often experience God in a way that I don't experience Him anywhere else. My understanding of my father and who He is expands exponentially when I am going through a trial.

1Peter 4:12-13 reminds us, "Dear friends, don't be surprise at the fiery trials you are going through, as if something strange were happening to you. Instead, be very glad – for these trial make you partners with Christ in his suffering".

Don't self deselect from the gift of a trial. Trust Him, lean on Him.

At times spiritual testing result in waves of spiritual refreshment. You can't have a testimony without a trial. Enjoy the read and the ride.

Hon. Vance D. Day
Former Circuit Court Judge
Third Judicial District (Oregon-USA)

CHAPTER 1

GENERAL INTRODUCTION - MISFORTUNE

Before we proceed properly into the first chapter of this book, we must first of all understand that in every part of the planet, there are good people and bad people. Also we must understand that misfortune befalls both good and bad people directly or indirectly both Christians and non Christians. When bad things happen to people, we hear statements like: where is God? Why did He allow such things to happen? Why some have out rightly concluded that there is no God.

A statement that is commonly used by insurance companies is "an act of God", which simply means that God was at fault or that He caused what happened. We understand that people say all kinds of things when they are angry or when there is a misfortune. Sometimes we say or do things that we later regret. Let's look at the meaning of the word misfortune.

MISFORTUNE:

The word "misfortune" means bad luck, an unfortunate condition or event. It could be a dead situation, in my opinion there were some people whom I would have never have wished for them to die, because they were so good and very helpful to

humanity. We know that no human is perfect but these kinds of people are to be described as angels in human form. Death is inevitable and how one dies is not in our hands but in the hands of God. This brings us to the question about the existence of God.

IS THERE GOD?

If there is a God, why does he permit or allow misfortune to befall good people? Of course in my opinion, there is God, the Almighty God. If we read "Psalm 24:1-10 and Genesis chapter one, it's enough to tell us that there is God, and He still exist. Science has made people to question the existence of God but mere looking around us an open minded person without any formal education can tell there is God. But some might choose to disbelieve or differ in their opinions about His existence, and they are entitled to theirs as well. As a Christian who believes in the Lord Jesus Christ and the Bible, I know that there is evil and there is good. I also know that there is God.

In the Book of "Psalm 14:1-3", it says that a fool has said that there is no God, they are corrupt, and not even one person is good upon the earth. Amongst many other proofs, the conception and the birth of a child is one of the mysteries of creation which must be attributed to God Almighty. Even if some don't believe, God is still

God regardless of our opinions. Going by the Oxford Dictionary meaning of the word "Good" it means that which is morally right, righteousness a mysterious balance of good and evil. All of us may have a different meaning of that word but if we go by the oxford dictionary, that person's character must be sound morally and of a good behavior.

Should misfortune or evil things happen to anyone? Didn't the Bible say in Matthew 5:45 that God sent sun and rain to fall on both the good and the evil people alike? Before conclude on why some people do bad or evil things, we should find out the meaning of those words. People do things that are punishable by death and afterward, feel sorry or remorseful, while others don't, and giving any space, they commit that same offence or evil again.

Why Do People Do Evil Things?

In order to establish why people commit or do what we consider as evil or wickedness, let's find the meaning of these words.

Evil/Wickedness:

Oxford Dictionary calls it a profound immorality and wickedness, especially when regarded as a supernatural force.

JEALOUSY:

Cambridge Dictionary says that it is a feeling of unhappiness and anger because someone has something or someone that you want. Judging from the above definitions, we can easily determine why people behave in a certain way not minding even taking somebody's life. If we value lives, we would be very careful, thoughtful and considerate before making decisions that will take somebody's life.

NOBODY IS PERFECT:

We will be looking deeply into the lives of some Bible characters and some of our spiritual and political leaders both past and present. Since no human is perfect we should be able to find something good in ones character that can be used as an example. God almighty gave every human being a conscience of knowing wrong and right, good and bad.

CHAPTER 2

JESUS CHRIST AND HIS CRUCIFIXION

The Bible explains in the book of Matthew, Mark, Luke and John the prophecy about His conception by the Holy Spirit, His birth and His Crucifixion and resurrection. The story of our Lord and savior Jesus Christ fills up the four gospels of the New Testament. We can only try extracting some undeniable and unmistakable facts that an innocent and a perfect individual were killed for being good. If we take time to read these four gospels, you will agree with the extract about Jesus Christ.

The Bible explains how He was conceived and born. Since there is no argument concerning that, and only a pagan would want to agree with empirical evidences contained in the Bible. I would like to lay emphasis in accordance with the title of the book-"Why does bad things happen to good people". The angel told Virgin Mary that she will be pregnant and that a son will be born and gave the name he will be called, and went on to list all the good things He will do for His people. From the moment Jesus was born, His life was in danger because a king name Herod was jealous of the newly born and planned to kill him. A child who was barely a week old was already an enemy to an evil and wicked king.

One does not need to offend someone before your life is attacked or killed. This is exactly what jealousy and wickedness does-without any provocation. While growing up He was never accused of wrong doing or anything unlawful. "Acts 10:38 tell us that:

How God anointed Jesus of Nazareth who went doing good and healing all those who were oppressed of the devil for God was with Him". Why should people want to kill someone who spent his whole life doing good?

Luke chapter 22:1-6:

The time was near for the festival of unleavened bread which is called a pass over, the chief priest and the teachers of the law were afraid of the people, and so they were trying to find a way of putting Jesus to death secretly. Why does one want to kill an innocent person who was only doing good things example: saving, healing, feeding the hungry multitude and protecting the weak?

WERE JUDAS ISCARIOT, KING HEROD AND CHIEF PRIESTS JEALOUS OF JESUS?

There could be no other logical reasons for this kind of hatred against an innocent individual.

If you dislike someone, you may not believe in him or her but you don't have to plan to kill them. Judas was the treasurer of Jesus ministry; he was in full control of all the funds of the ministry. The way he spent the funds was never questioned by Jesus Christ. Why did he betray his master and Lord? "Luke 22:3-6 recorded this fact:

Satan entered Judas Iscariot, who was one of the twelve disciples. He went off and spoke with chief priests and the officers of the temple about how he would betray Jesus to them. They were pleased and offer to pay him money. Judas agreed to the plan and from that moment he began to look for opportunity to betray Jesus to them.

It is interesting to learn that Satan, that is evil spirit took over Judas to do what he did. A normal rational person would have considered that Jesus had given him a job of controlling his money for his ministry. Jesus was innocent and a sinless man. This action of Judas confirms what Apostle Paul said in "1 Timothy6:10 – For the love of money is the source of all kinds of evil. Some have been so eager to have it that they have wandered from the faith and have broken many hearts with many sorrows."

So we can conclude that good people suffers in the hands of wicked and evil people all over the world, and also in the Bible. In conclusion let us look into the testimonies of three individual about Jesus Christ.

1. Matthew 19:16-17

    The wealthy man said to Jesus, good master, what good thing do I need to do so I can have eternal life. That must be the reason why he referred to Jesus Christ as good.

2. Matthew 27:19

    While Pontius Pilate was sitting to judge Jesus, his wife sent a message warning him that Jesus Christ was innocent because she had a dream. She warned her husband that the one standing in front of him was an innocent man.

Pilate said to chief priests, and the crowd I find no reason to condemn this man.

3. Matthew 27: 3-11
    Judas Iscariot himself said:

    When Judas saw that Jesus was condemned, he repented and brought back the thirty pieces of silver to the chief priests and the elders and said, I have sinned because I had betrayed the innocent blood.

Innocent people all over the world are being persecuted, tortured and killed every day. If you are one of those who had engaged or engaging in this kind of evil, you can still repent. There is no repentance in the grave. Jesus Christ forgave those who crucified Him and He will do the same for us because no man is perfect, when we sin we ask for forgiveness and He will abundantly pardon.

CHAPTER 3

JOSEPH AND HIS BROTHERS

– Genesis 37 to 50

In order to fully understand the story about Joseph the son of Jacob we need to read above chapters in the book of Genesis but because I have read them several times, I will try to summarize them. Joseph had eleven brothers from one father whose name is Jacob, the son of Isaac. Joseph was the eleventh son and his father Isaac loved him very much perhaps more than others. He was very obedient and respectful to both his parents and siblings. His father had a soft spot for him and bought a coat of many colors i.e. beautiful coat and his brothers did not like the fact that their father favored Joseph.

One day, while he was 17th years old, he had a dream that could be described as upliftment, increase and influence and his brothers did not like when he shared the dream with them. After that he had another dream which could be described as Lordship over them and they hated him more and became jealous of their junior brother. Joseph's brothers were shepherds by profession and one day his father sent him to take food to his brothers and to know how they were doing. As an obedient child, wearing the coat his father made for him could have fueled the intensity of their hatred, jealousy and anger.

When they saw him coming, they scoffed at him by calling him "A DREAMER" and conspired to kill their innocent brother who came to bring food to them. They kidnapped, mistreated and wanted to kill him to see how he can realize the dream, but one of his brothers named Ruben pleaded with others not to kill him but instead to sell him into slavery to the merchants heading to Egypt.

"WHY DOES BAD THINGS HAPPENS TO GOOD PEOPLE"

This 17th year old did not commit any offence for having dreams and sharing them with his family. Jealousy not checked can turn to wickedness and evil. Joseph suffered multiple rejections; cover up, false accusation and imprisonment caused by his brothers for being a good person and being an obedient child to his parents. Joseph's brothers lied to their parents that a wild animal had killed Joseph; to cover up they killed an animal and soaked his coat in blood so that their parents will believe that a wild animal had killed Joseph. Jacob mourned for his son believing that he had been killed as his sons reported to him. How evil can a jealous mind go? I could not imagine the agony and pain he must have endured.

Thirteen years later at the age of thirty years this dream finally happened by being able to interpret the dream of the king of Egypt Pharaoh. God gave Joseph the meaning of the dream which none of the astrologers, magicians and suit Sayers who work for the king could not interpret. The king appointed Joseph as the Prime minster in Egypt as the deputy to pharaoh in all Egypt entrusting him with the wealth of the country. He became the second most important, famous and important and influential man in all Egypt. Casting our mind back, Joseph's dream was fulfilled as he shared to his family.

FOOD WAS PLENTY IN EGYPT:

At that time of extreme famine in Canaan and surrounding nations, people all were coming into Egypt to purchase food and Joseph was solely in control of all the supplies. Jacob had heard that there was plenty of food in Egypt and he asked his children to travel to Egypt to buy food so the whole family will not die of starvation. Neither Jacob nor his children knew that the man in charge in Egypt was Joseph. You would enjoy this incredible story of God's divine plan and promotion if you would take time to read those chapters in Genesis.

When the brothers arrived in the country Joseph recognized them but they did not – recognize their brother Joseph. The evil that people commit do catch up with them alive or dead. Joseph must have acted very well not to have revealed himself at first; I could imagine what must have been racing through his heart. The hatred, betrayal, torture, slavery, attempted murder must have been flashed through his mind. Who need siblings like those? He kept his composure and ordered his men to serve his brothers.

Are you beginning to wonder how this story ended? I would have loved to stop here but the story of a 17th year old having a dream and paying a huge price for it wouldn't have been completed. Joseph believed in his dream and was prepared to suffer and die for it. The Bible said in Genesis 39:2- 4, "AND GOD WAS WITH JOSEPH". It was a story of trusting in God, belief and tenacity. Do you believe in your dream? Is your dream from God?

When Joseph saw his brothers, he remembered the dreams he had dreamt because his brothers bowed down to him. Joseph asked his brothers who they were, where they came from and about their parents. At this time, he knew that his father and his junior brother Benjamin were alive. They carried the food that they have bought and returned to Canaan but Joseph accused one of them of stealing so he could hold one of his brothers back with him in Egypt knowing that they will come back to buy more food.

Joseph excused himself and wept when he realized that his father and junior brother were still alive. Jacob sent back his children back to Egypt to buy more food but this time with Benjamin because Joseph had requested that he must accompany them if they must be attended to. He wanted to see Benjamin after 13years of being absent from the family.

Joseph instructed his servants to prepare for lunch with his brothers at his home on their second visit to Egypt. With mixed emotions Joseph revealed himself to his brothers and they bowed down their faces before Joseph, which again was the fulfillment of the dreams he had 13years earlier. The brothers were afraid of retributions from Joseph but he said to them "You planned evil against me but God meant it for good so I can save you people's lives. He asked his brothers to go and bring the whole family to Egypt so he can save their lives from starvation. The king of Egypt Pharaoh instructed Joseph to provide a place for his family and wagons were sent by Joseph to convey the whole clan to Egypt. He relocated the family to a place called Goshen so they could be near him. Jacob hugged Joseph and wept on his shoulder and said, I can die now in peace seeing that my son whom I thought was dead is alive.

This was the true story of a boy who became a man of power and influence through negative circumstances orchestrated by his wicked and jealous brothers. He forgave his brothers because God kept him alive and he became a blessing to many people within and outside Egypt. This is the story of bad things happening to a good man.

CHAPTER 4

❧❧❧❧❧❧ ❧❧❧❧❧❧

THE THIEF IN OUR CHURCH

Since the inception of the church – Zion Praise Centre International Church, we have been helping in our community such as the alcoholics, drug addicts, the homeless folks. Some of them we bring into the Church pray and offer free counseling without which some would have committed suicide. Even if they committed offence and sent to prison, we go and visit and offer any support that they need.

In our December thanksgiving service, our church women will cook for all of them and sometimes we book a restaurant in town and take then to eat. This practice had become an annual event until the inevitability occurred. On Sunday 8th December 2015, a young Scottish white man walked into the morning service, he was well received. He informed me that he was hungry. After the church service we prayed for him, gave him food and a Bible. He further informed me he did not have heater where he was staying that he didn't have money for gas, we gave him money to put gas in his heating system. This was not new to us because we face this kind of situation all the time. We encourage him to come back for evening service because we noticed that he was depressed and to our surprise he came back. Some of such people don't come back until they need another help.

After the service a member of the church took him out to buy food for him and his dog. We found out that according to him, that his dog had not eaten all day. While they were at the store buying food for this guy, he stole something from the shop and the church member saw it and forced him to replace the stolen item. This man went home with food for himself and the dog. The church building locked and everyone gone home. This guy came back in the night and climbed the roof broke two windows and smashed the office door and stole £1000 that was raised for our church mission in Nigeria – Africa. When I came to the office on Monday morning, there were broken glasses and blood stains on the windows and door. I was shocked to see what I saw, having been here not less than 24 hours before. I went to the Kirkcaldy police station and made a report. The police asked me if I had a suspect and my thought went to the guy we had helped last night. I gave his name to the police and his address where he was staying. The police did a wonderful job, they sent in a forensic guy and a lady. They took the blood samples and in a day the result was out and they brought some pictures for identification.

I confirmed the suspect and the police confirmed that he was the one who committed the crime and that was not his first time of committing such crime. I was told by the police that a report had been sent to the procurator physical and recommended that the £1000 should be refunded to the church.

INJUSTICE OR DISCRIMINATION:

The case was charged to court in Kirkcaldy and I was notified of the date. On the court day I went to the court but I was not allowed to seat in the hearing. When I questioned why I was told that it was close hearing. This was the decision of the judge I was told. I asked my lawyer if the church would be compensated and the answer was no. How can this be justice? To bear the loss of £1000 and the damage to the property? I this incident had occurred to the court building; will the judge give the same judgment? Will this man not to be punished?

The church prayed and committed this case to God Almighty to judge. The judge might have used his power against us, but the heavenly judge has final say in this matter.

This guy came to me after few days to beg and asked for forgiveness and I forgave him that is the reason his name is withheld. So, his identity is not made public. The social worker moved him out of town. Is this injustice or discrimination or both? I remember this almost every day whenever I enter the office, although the windows have been replaced but the door have not been replaced. I would not have supported a prison sentence, but the church money as recommended by the police should have been refunded. That action by the judge has affected the way we treat the needy in our community. We will never place ourselves in such condition ever again.

CHAPTER 5

THE POPES AND
THEIR LIFESTYLE

My upbringing is Roman Catholic and I am very proud of this background. I lived and served the priests in town called Ihiala – Anambra State, Nigeria I worked in the church as an altar boy. I had learned some great and wonderful things which are still very useful to me in our ministry. The Roman Catholic Church is as old as it could get – the early church and in its history have had 266 popes till date.

I see that position as a sacred and divine. The level of sacrifices the Pope makes are enormous yet people still criticize them ignorantly. The Popes are not perfect and they are human beings and are born by mothers. When I was very young, I actually saw them as gods who were dropped down from heaven. We shall be able to look into some of the sacrifices that shaped their lives. So many people do not give them the respect they deserve. I am not talking about worshipping or idolizing them. Only the Father, the Son and the Holy Spirit are to be worshipped. I am a Pentecostal preacher but am proud of my Catholic Childhood and do not mean I don't have issues with some of the teachings of the church, of course I do. I will not discuss the church but the pontiff.

In 2025 our current Pope is His Holiness Pope Francis, was (born Jorge Mario Bergoglio – 17th December 1936) The 266 current Pope of Roman Catholic Church. He is 88years and was born in Flore Buenos Aires, Argentina. I will try to make a little comparison with other men of God from other denomination especially the Pentecostal preachers. It is horrible for anybody to call the Pope an antichrist. If that was a case the anti-Christ must have come and gone, because we have had 266 of them. Whatever criticism they receive they don't reply nor respond but instead they pray for that person or group. Please bear in mind that they are not perfect, they go through pain as everyone else but due to training in seclusion, they receive it as Christ would. A normal Pentecostal Bishop will course you from his pulpit. Some Pastors when members leave their church, they do something that is unprintable. All the Popes are intelligent and versatile individuals.

Our current Pope Francis is fluent in Spanish, Italian, German, French, Portuguese and English. They are very humanitarian and sincerely love the poor. I am very worried when they are unjustly malign and falsely fabricate stories against.

Why do bad things happen to good people? Comparing the Popes with other men of God in other denominations:

1. They give up their birth rights
2. They don't have money; the money belongs to the Catholic Church.
3. They don't have personal home; the Vatican belongs to the church.

4. They do not get married, sworn to celibacy.

5. They don't have a personal vehicle; the bullet proof car does not belong to either of them just like the plane. Nothing really belongs to them. When they die, they are not buried in the country of their birth or in family grave. Job described it perfectly, naked you came, and naked you leave. Beside the reward you believe and intend to receive from God, they do not have any earthly possession they could leave their family.

When Pope Benedict has health challenges, he resigned so the cardinals could choose a replacement. In other religious organizations like the Pentecostal the man will remain until he dies or appoint either his wife or children to take over in order to protect the family empire, whether the person is called by God or not. I am against the family serving or working in the church but a family owing a church is unscriptural. Jesus Christ did not do that and the Apostle did not do it. We cannot blame those criticize the church as a business.

HOW POPES ARE APPOINTED

If we look into how these men were appointed or selected, there is no other religious organization that has a disciplined and meticulous program. The College of Cardinals known as the papal conclave locks themselves into a chapel for prayers and deliberations no matter how long it takes until a replacement or successor is selected amongst themselves. This is very impressive. This is not determined by age or by year of ordination, not by the country of birth nor your race.

If the black smoke come up it signifies that they haven't found a successor and that means they remain inside until one is chosen and only then will the white smoke come up. Some people may call that and old tradition. A very good old tradition. The Bible is very old.

The Pontiff lives extra ordinary sacrificial life. They are not paid salary but well looked after by the church, so they can serve God and humanity. Why would someone want to harm such men? They are not politicians. They are not perfect but good men who have devoted their lives for serving God. I may not agree with everything the church believes in, but I respect them very much. These are my views as an ex catholic boy.

CHAPTER 6

PRESIDENT DONALD J. TRUMP AS A WINNER

The oxford Dictionary described the word winner as "A goal or shot that wins a match or point, he equalized and hit a last-minute winner".

This definition clearly describes the president, his style of leadership and the way he won the November 5th 2024 election. That is what we call in Scotland a "Die hard Spirit" It's a spirit that makes a leader who sticks to an opinion and follows it through no matter what. Maybe it is because President Trump has a Scottish blood in him.

He manifested that spirit for the world to see during his assassination attempt during the campaign. Such character is what Apostle Paul described in "2Corinthians 4:8-9. We are often troubled but not crushed, sometimes in doubt, but never in despair, there are many enemies, but we are never without a friend and though badly hurt at times, we are not destroyed". When you listen to the team which the president has assembled to work with him, people like Hon. Speaker Mike Johnson, Pam Bondi, Marco Rubio and others, that spirit of Maga is on all of them. The world watched a man who was bleeding badly and he was still in his fighting spirit because he loves his county.

I believe so strongly that the re-emergence and the victory of Mr. Trump was an "act of God" allow me to borrow the insurance company's phrase. That kind of spirit is infectious. I don't understand why anyone would want to kill a man because he loves and want to serve his country. There is absolutely nothing wrong with a man who wants his country to be great again. President is not perfect and has never claimed to be, just like all of us. No human can ever be perfect in the sight of Almighty God.

The Bible tells us that only God is perfect and God had never used a perfect person to fulfill His plans because there is none. The greatest apostle of the New Testament was Paul, and he boldly declared in "1 Corinthian 1:27-29 – God purposely choose what the world considers nonsense in order to shame the wise, and he choose what the world considers weak in order to shame the powerful. He chooses what the world looks down on and despises and think is nothing in order to destroy what the world thinks is important. This means that no one can boast in God's presence

I believe that Trump can perfectly fit into this scripture. He is hated, dislike, accused by his enemies but the American people love him and proved it on November 5th 2024. Jesus Christ who God sent to the world was hated by His enemies who constantly sought ways to kill Him.

IS PRESIDENT TRUMP A CHRISTIAN?

Absolutely yes in my opinion and the opinion of the Bible "Romans 10:9 says, that "if you confess with the Lord Jesus and believe in your heart that God has raised Him from the dead, you will be saved". Has Mr. President not done that? I have read articles from people who accuse him of just pretending so that Christians who vote for him. Now that he is the President, he is still professing Jesus Christ as Lord. After all, it is Jesus Christ who Know those who are his.

I have heard him few times say that "God preserves his life so he can make America great again". To that I would add "make the world better again". As a citizen of free world and Christian, I am grateful to God that Mr. Trump is the President of the free world. This is a heavy responsibility that only very few people in the world can handle. This is why every Christian should pray for him as the Bible says in 1Thimothy 2:1-3. If you are a Christian, you will be failing in your duties if don't pray for him. God is neither a Democrat nor a Republican – therefore you don't have to be a Republican in order to pray for your President. I am not a Muslim but I pray for our Nigerian President Bola Ahmed Tinubu and United Kingdom Prime Minister RT. Hon. Keir Starmer, as the Bible instructed. I don't have to belong to their parties for me to do that as a believer in Christ Jesus.

The way our world is headed, I will believe God will use President Trump to direct and re-direct some things that have been wrong for so long. In his first term as President, he was a novice but he is experience and ready for the job with God's help. He has great minds in JD VANCE, CHUCK GRASSLEY, JOHN THUNE and MIKE

JOHNSON. With the advantages of having the majorities in both House and Senate, the sky will be the limit.

10 REASONS WHY PRESIDENT TRUMP WON!

I am not an American but I know he was going to win, I told my American friends and I sent a letter to the Trump Tower in New York, before the election.

1. He won the first attempt as the President while a novice, the second attempt he believed it was taken away from him, and his opponent was not a strong one.
2. He had learnt from the lost attempt.
3. He saw problems of the people and offered them a solution.
4. He campaigned based on what was happening in the country and around the world .eg Wars.
5. He compared his first term achievement to his predecessor and know what he would improve on if re-elected'
6. He used a powerful slogan "Make American Grate Again" The people caught and ran with it. It sounded positive and promising.
7. He capitalized on the statistics of the events in the country. eg Immigration and crime.
8. The attempt on his life made people thinking.
9. He chose the right people to campaign with and for him.
10. More churches were praying for him and with the help of God almighty, he is now the President of America!

CHAPTER 7

VICTMIZATION BY THE AUTHORITIES

My upbringing was peaceful and lovely amongst ten other siblings. Brought up in a Christian home by a male father who was a police officer and a teacher and a female mother who was a semi-trader and a farmer Living in Nigeria none of my brother and sisters ever gotten into any trouble with the law. Lived and served the priests in the seminary, desiring that one day I would be a priest.

Finally, when I later become a minister in the Pentecostal organization, it was not a surprise to many who saw me growing up under the tutelage of the Priests. Our parents never allowed us to fight with each other or outside the house. So, I have a mind that if I ever decide not to be a priest and have children, we will make sure that they receive the same upbringing I had from our parents.

When I came to United Kingdom in 1986, I was given a visa that forbade me from engaging in any type of employment paid or unpaid. It was tough for me, my friends were working but I refuse to violate the law even when a Christian brother offered me a job in his company, I turned it down. When I got married and we began to have children my wife and I decided that as Christians, we would train our children in a proper manner which includes no drinking, smoking and of cause no fighting.

At this period in 2014 our children Joseph was 11years while Jessica was 10years and both of them were attending Our Lady's Primary School in Sterling-Scotland. They were both enjoying the school where they had made good friends. In 2014 on Friday, I heard a shout from both of them and I realized that they were fighting, I rushed down stairs and rolled a daily newspaper which I read that morning and smacked both of them twice on their bottom as a correction, since they were warned not to fight with each other, they apologized and that was it and they never fought against each other and both are in the university.

Another occasion our son Joseph misbehaved at home and his mother disciplined him by smacking as a means of correction and on getting to school the teacher was asking the class how happy they were during the weekend. An 11years old boy mentioned to the teacher the discipline he received at home form mom. A mischievous teacher began to probe and reported it to the head teacher and head teacher contacted the social worker and the police was invited.

They took our son into a private room and began to question him if his dad anytime hit him; he told them that dad had at some time hit him and sister.

I had stated that I did and the reason and they believed that we had abused our children. At this time our daughter didn't know what was happening because she was in her own classroom. She was brought in after their evil plan was concluded that our children were not coming home that day.

The Police, head teacher and the social worker waited until school closing time when all the parents were around to collect their children before they informed our children that they would not be going home with their mother who brought them to school that morning. Was this not racism? Was this not evil? Please think this over if you may, you dropped off your children at school in the morning and you return at school closing time to be told that your children were not going home with you because you have been abusing them.

There was no single evidence whatsoever. I was on a trip to Nigeria on charity mission feeding the hungry children and was to return to Scotland that same day. It was totally not true that we were abusing our children.

RACIAL DESCRIMINATION:

On arrival in the country my wife and I were invited by police at different times for questioning. I contacted my lawyer she advise me to proceed to the station to make a statement. In my statement I confirmed that I had on occasion disciplined our children with a rolled daily newspaper. We were both reminded in police cell at different times. By this time our children had been placed in the home of two white lesbian women to foster our children. Our African culture is completely different from Scotland. The head teacher, police and the social worker had achieved their aim against us without any warning our children were gone to two white lesbian women. In all my 36years of residing in Scotland and doing charity work as a minster, that was my most painful experiences in my life.

I can never forget the year 2014/15 in a hurry, the country I loved. I started regretting why I came to Scotland instead of going to United States when I had many opportunities. But I knew I was called to Scotland by God as a missionary. Our children were traumatized living in home of lesbians; this was not our culture and one of the women worked at our Lady's Primary School where our children attend in Sterling. These tried everything to confuse and convince our children that they will be good parents to them. They bought expensive thing for them, promised to take them on an exotic holiday to different countries. When the women told our children that they will be staying with them until they turn 16years at least, my daughter would cry and my heart was broken. I could not sleep; I would stay up at night thinking and praying. The Scottish children reporter got involved and different meetings were arranged on how we can see how children once in two weeks under social worker supervisions. After every visit was the worst, our children would cry holding us not to leave them. We kept assuring them that we would take this group to court and they would come home.

God was with us and He gave us a good layer. On every supervised visit our children would tell us how difficult it has been for them staying with the ladies. Our children told them that the Bible did not support their relationship as two women and they would respond that God made them the way they were. Our children were Christians and their parents were ministers so they know what the Bible says. Our children were denied the types of African foods they were used to eating. They lost so much weight for noting the proper food they were used to.

CHILDREN HEARING:

We began to attend the children's hearing meetings with the panel whom were to make decisions concerning our children and all members of the panel were white. How are we supposed to trust based on what we were going through to that point? For the sake of our children, we diligently attended every meeting, sometimes with our lawyer. The children's Reporter wrote in his supporting facts. a-Between 1st January 2010 and April 24th 2014, exact date unknown, Mrs. Nwokoye hit Joseph on his hands with a spoon as chastisement for misbehaving.

b- In April 2014, exact date unknown, Mr. Nwokoye hit Joseph and Jessica on their buttocks with a rolled piece of cardboard.

They concluded that a crime had been committed. We decided that the case should go to court. Our lawyer made sure it should go to court. Our lawyer made sure it went to court because were unfairly treated.

At the court, both lawyers presented their cases, our children were not allowed to attend due to their ages. We prayed so much because we knew it was us against the authorities, but God became the judge. I will hear of our children in my head even if I was seating down or on the pulpit preaching. It was a torture for me. I would ask myself, how can trying to raise good children be a crime in Scotland. I went physical, psychological and spiritual pain.

THE JUDGEMENT DAY

The date came for the judge to deliver the judgment. The court was packed and tensed. The judge took his time to explain the actions of all the parties involved in the case from the beginning. The Police, School, social work, children's reporter, my wife and I. Finally, he came to his conclusion:

"I conclude now that it is no longer necessary for them to be in foster care and they should now be returned immediately.

We didn't know how to rejoice, whether to cry or smile after so much pain. God fought this battle for us. We thanked and hugged our lawyer who stood by us. Our children were taken away from us at the school; we went to school straight away from the court to collect our children back from the school. We do not and will never support any parent or persons abusing the children. But the Bible which is what we believe in as Christians encourages parent to "Train a child the way he should go when he is old, he will not depart from it – Proverbs 22:6". "And he who spares his rod hates his son, but he who loves him discipline him promptly – Proverbs 13: 24".

The streets of Scotland are full of undisciplined children that the government cannot control. When you remove Christ from your schools, you invite crisis and that's what we are experiencing on daily basis on our streets unfortunately. In one of his speeches, President Donald J. Trump encouraged the Americans to have a Bible in their homes. Great Britain without God will be a time bomb waiting to explode.

CHAPTER 8

A GOOD MAN WHO
SUFFERED FOR GOD

The book of Job in the Bible teaches us about a man named Job who went through the good, the bad and the tragedies. Not many people can pass through what Job went through and remain same. This a man whom the Bible described as a "Perfect and righteous man" Genesis Chapter 1:27, tells us that God created human beings to be like him, made them male and female and God blessed them. Then man sinned and everything changed.

WHO WAS JOB?

There was a man named Job, living in the land of Uz, who worshipped God and was faithful to Him. He was a good man, very careful not to do anything evil. We are talking about a good man who suffered total disaster. He loses all his ten children, all his wealth, was afflicted with an incurable disease and in the mist of all these calamities, his wife rejected him and told he better be dead than alive. Apart from our Lord Jesus Christ, Job was probably was the next human who went through an imaginable crisis ever recorded in any book. Job's story tells us that good people are not exempted from bad things happening to them. The Bible tells us that God confirmed that Job was a good man, who respected God and worshipped Him. Why then do bad things happen to a good man? The origin of evil things is Satan, whether we are Christians or not, for example, when someone is under the influence of a substance, that person can end up in prison.

This simply means that he or she was being controlled by another thing. In John chapter 13, we read that "Satan entered into Judas Iscariot's mind to betray his master but as soon as his mind was cleared, he immediately became remorseful and returned the proceed of his evil act but it was too late. Whenever people commit a heinous crime, they usually claim that Satan made them do it. But in the case of Job God allowed it so that He could confirm what He said about Job and to get the glory out of the trial. The ways and manner he handled his adversities, the way he responded to his wife insult on his integrity confirmed what God had said about Job although he was still human. Many of us will stop attending church, stop serving God and may even confess that there was no God if we had gone through one percent of what Job went through. It is clearly recorded that Job did not sin against God with his mouth but instead worshipped God. How can one be able to do that, unless one had an intimate, unbreakable, undivided and solid relationship with his/her God?

Even our Lord and Savior Jesus Christ at Gethsemane felt the pain of sins on Him.

THE RESTORATION OF JOB'S FORTUNE:

After all the trials he made these confessions "Job chapter 19:25-27 I know that my redeemer lives and that in the end He will stand on the earth. And after my skin has been destroyed, yet in my flesh I will see God. I myself will see Him with my eyes, how my heart yearns within me". This is incredible coming from a man who was destroyed by Satan but God confirmed that Job has passed the test. You and I may one day be tested in a different way, but would we be able to stand the test, without sinning with our mouth against God. May God help us in this terrible world to be able to stand the test? The Bible recorded the latter part of Job's life like this: "Job chapter 42:10-16. The after Job had prayed for his friends, the Lord made him prosperous again and gave twice as much as he had before. All Job's brothers and sisters and former friends came to visit him and feasted in his house. They expressed their sympathy and comforted him for all the troubles the Lord had allowed to befall him. Each brought money and gold. The Lord blessed the last part of Job's life more than before.

Job lived up to 140 years after this and saw his great grandchildren and he died a very old man. What way to end one's life.

CHAPTER 9

PROTECTING INNOCENT CHILDREN FROM ABDUCTION AND ASSAULT

These two chapters of the Bible should summarize this chapter we are about to read. "James chapter 1:17 every good gift and every perfect gift is from above, and cometh down from the father of lights, with whom is no variableness neither shadow of turning". "Psalm 127:3 children are a gift from the Lord; they are a reward from Him". Children are assault and abduction is a new thing in the world, it has been in existence since wickedness and slavery began. Every evil thing that is being perpetuated on earth originated from Satan. This book is written in order to help shine light on why bad things happen to good people, which refers largely to children who are innocent and vulnerable in most cases. My intention is not to force the reader become a Christian or to start attending a church, but alert us about the dangers our children face and how to avoid them.

Parents and guardians must be willing to sacrifice time and also be discussing with their children. This is why education so vital today more than ever, and informed parent will not be easily misinformed.

For instance, many years ago, some white people did not believe that there was racism in their community. A racist would not accept that he is one until proven otherwise. It goes into the blood of our society and has become a cancer that is spreading. Even children are practicing racism that is not good for our society, children being introduced to such a terrible act. Every parent and guardians should judge their conscience, are you a racist?

WHAT IS CHILD ABUSE?

What some people consider as an abuse could be normal to others. Abuse is a physical, verbal, sexual or emotional mistreatment of a child that is motivated by anger. One can trick a child into false love while abusing them secretly. In some cases, children who were abused often grow up to be an abuser themselves. Every parent or guardian at one point feels angry and frustrated when their children misbehave, disobey, insult, or talk back on them. Sometimes we are tired after a long day at work and we just want them to do what they were asked to do, and if they don't we snap and sometimes get out of control. But that shouldn't be an excuse for an abuse, we must learn self-control.

ABUCTION AND MOLESTATION:

Children want to feel save in the hands of their parents and guardian and it's their God given right. I had always felt very save in company of my parents as a child, you will feel so protected as if nothing can happen to you, I noticed that with my own children also. Years ago, parents' primary job was to watch that children don't injure themselves in a playground or with a sharp object, but responsibilities have increased to protecting children from possible molestation and abduction. Our eyes are always watching out to know where they are, who are they with and if they are older, we call on phone, text or E-mail to check on them. Some parents/ guardians are naive as to the subtle and divisive ways child molesters and abductors think and operate. Do not think that it won't happen to your child instead begin to teach them young as they can understand. We should tell them how to say no to strangers, not to accept gifts, sweet or money without your consent. Not to sit on the laps of the one you don't approve whether they are family members or church members. Because of the dangers of our generations, that is why you have CCTV cameras almost in anywhere imaginable. At the airport, streets, shopping malls, sports stadium for protection. Our children should not trust the people we don't trust, they need to be thought, trained in every way possible.

THESE ARE SOME WAYS PARENTS ENDANGER THEIR CHILDREN

a) Ephesians 6:1-3, children obey your parents in the Lord, for this is right. Honour your father and mother which is the first commandment with promise that it may be well with you and you may live long on the earth. While it is good for children to obey, they should think what not to obey, for example, if a teacher, doctor, pastor, family member wants them to touch or be touched in an inappropriate way, they must say no and report it to the appropriate authority.

b) PARENT PLEASE TO YOUR CHILDREN

If we train them, we know when and if they are telling the truth or lying. We don't want our children to accuse someone wrongly and get in trouble. We must know them, ask them questions and study their body language, find out who their friends are and the kind of homes they come from. Our son once told me that his football coach smokes a lot, sometimes inside the mini bus that conveys them and the coach swears just like his father. That was the end of the football training and him playing for that team. We didn't want our kid in that of environment.

c) PARENTS BE YOUR CHILDREN'S FRIEND:

If our children see us as their friends, they will tell us anything. There are things about me that my friends know which my siblings don't know. We tend to open up to our friends than family. Have you told a friend something and ask them not to tell anybody? We forgot that our friends also have their own best friends that you may not know. While growing up, we did not discuss any sexual issues with parents and guardians if not they would discuss it with the wrong persons.

d) PARENTS, PLEASE HUG YOUR CHILDREN:

Some parents are afraid that if they hug, cuddle or kiss their children especially teens that the children would be embarrassed in front of their friends or may be accused of incest. If we were doing it when they were small as babies, they would not be embarrassed, instead they know it's a sign of love and godly affection. If you know your child well, you will know when they need a hug or kiss. When our two 10 and 11 years old were forced into foster care, they missed our hugs and kisses so much that they would hug us and let go whenever we see them during our supervised visits. They would ask their mum to put bright red lip stick kisses on their school jumpers and coats. At the end of every contact visit, we would carry them on our backs from the room to where the foster ladies or the social workers car were packed. We would cuddle together sometimes on the couch covered duvet to watch TV together. Some children would feel rejected if their parents stop hugging them. At a certain age kisses must stop but hugs would continue. Molesters can stop signs of vulnerability of a child if a child is withdrawn or depressed due to a feeling of rejection, that child could be a target for molesters.

CHILDREN NEED THE PROTECTION OF ADULTS:

a) Watch out for them at all times if they are still at home, don't leave them alone in the car while shopping, or in a public place alone. The world is no longer the way it's used to be.

b) Don't place your child's name on his or her school bags or books. It may give a potential abductor opportunity to know your child's name. A child who hears his or her name called by a stranger may engage in conversation with stranger.

c) Take several photographs of your child both in school uniforms and casual clothes; it will help you if he or she happens to be missing. Children who can speak and write can be taught emergency numbers, home address, and full names of parents, town or city they live in and police contacts.

d) Give the school teacher, head teacher or principal power to notify the parents or guardians if your child did not report to school. If your child said that they were going to camp or youth group, the leader should notify you if he or she didn't show up.

e) You must try to find out who their friends are and subsequently their parents. Be careful how you allow your child to a sleep over at a friend's house. When you do allow a sleep over, find out what they will be doing and watching. Some children have access to stranger via social-media in their bedrooms.

f) Finally, you must pray for them and leave the rest to God, who knows what we don't know and see what we don't see.

SOME SIGNS OF SEXUAL ABUSE IN CHILDREN:

As parents or guardians, we need to be watchful of these signs in our children.

I) Appears to be withdrawn suddenly.

II) Begins to perform poorly in school and a suddenly change in their class grade or result.

III) A sudden change in appetite without being sick/ill.

IV) Becomes sexually promiscuous or provocative in the way he or she dresses.

V) Engages in excessive and compulsive masturbation.

VI) Suddenly an unannounced run away from home and will not tell anybody of his/her destination.

CHAPTER 10

A MAN OF INTEGRITY - PRESIDENT NELSON MANDELA

Born on the 18th July 1918 in Mvezo village, an area called Transanskic in South Africa. He was a trained lawyer by profession, an anti-apartheid activist and a philanthropist. As a proud African, I refer to him as "Papa Mandela, he was a father to Africa. My late father was born in 1917, so to refer to him as father is an act of a great respect. You have to deserve it for me to call you, my father.

His deep love for his people landed him in prison. He campaigned against injustice, and victimization against blacks. The government of South Africa arrested him in 1962 accusing him of trying to overthrow the government. How can a young man with no military might overthrow a government that controls the military and the Amory of the nation.

Following the Rivonia trial, he was sentenced to life imprisonment. He suffered torture and inhumane act by the apartheid government. I renamed apartheid the junior brother of slave trade; the only difference was that money does not exchange hands. During the 27years imprisonment, he was moved around between three prisons namely Victor Verster Prison, Pollsmoor Prison and Robin Island. If the government knew or envisaged that sending him to prison would make him a hero to world, they wouldn't have. People go prison for committing a crime or an offence but going to prison for trying to do what is good is unforgettable.

THE GOSPEL OF LOVE AND FORGIVENESS:

President Mandela was released from prison amidst heavy protest, and severe international pressures from different organizations on the 11th February 1990. He came out from prison with what I called "The gospel of love and forgiveness". He forgave all those who were against him, he beard no bitterness or hatred instead he focused on reconciling the country. All of humanity should learn from this great man what the Bible said in Mark 11:25-26 "Jesus Christ said forgiven but if you do not forgive, God will not forgive of your sins".

His behavior and action to forgive touched me greatly as a preacher of the gospel. Volumes can be written of this great human being. President F. W. De Klerk was the leader in South Africa when he was released.

He rejoined in active politics under African Nation Congress (A.N.C) and contested for the presidential election and won. He was sworn in on the 10th of May 1994 as the country's first black president. He led the party and the country from 1994 to 1999. He negotiated with other political parties to end apartheid and established a multiracial government. In 1993 the Nobel Peace Prize was awarded jointly to President Nelson Mandela and President F. W. De Klerk for their work for a peaceful South African. I sincerely pray and wish that our African leaders will emulate this great leader who did not abuse this office to avenge his so-called enemies, as the Commander in Chief, he could have what he wanted.

He did not use his position to amass illegal wealth; he could have if he wanted to enrich himself. I am not from South Africa but I wept when he died and when I read about what he left in his will, I concluded he was that preserved by God to serve his people and left a legacy for the coming leaders. From prison to presidency just like the story of Joseph the sun of Jacob in the Bible. From prison to Prime Minister and forgave his brothers who hated him and treated him badly. President Nelson Mandela was not perfect like every one of us, but he was a good and great man. May his soul rest in perfect peace

www.ingramcontent.com/pod-product-compliance
Lightning Source LLC
Chambersburg PA
CBHW020422150626
46554CB00014B/2382